WHERE I WAS BORN

poems

Naoko Fujimoto

Where I Was Born

Editor: Randall Horton

Cover art: Minami Kobayashi

Author photo: Gail Goepfert

ISBN 978-1-7322091-8-3

LCCN 2019934836

Willow Books, a Division of Aquarius Press

www.WillowLit.net

Printed in the United States of America

Contents

For Takeshi Fujimoto

POCHI OR KURO

Following
the ghost dog down, Father implanted a stroke.
It is resting in my great uncle's
side of the graveyard with people I had
never talked to. Mother said, "The dog should not be here.
Bad luck for ancestors and descendants." Father used to say,
"It ate its own shit." Its name was forgotten; Pochi or
Kuro, a common Japanese dog's name. When
Father jogged in the morning, the dog
waited by the telephone pole. It barked,
and Father replied, "I am struggling with a new
computer system." The dog sniffed
his hand as if saying, *I smell nappa-cabbage.* It licked
him three times, *Don't drive today.*
You partial, vegetable.

A NARROW SQUARE

He had never slapped anything.
Even he did not kill a long-legged

wasp carrying spring dirt. He poked it
with a flyswatter and said, "Mr. Bee…"

Mother ordered, "Kill it now,"
and brought pesticide.

We used to live on the fifteenth
floor, but we occasionally had wasps.

Sister and I tossed dolls, colored pencils,
and gumballs over the balcony.

When we could not find things to toss,
we climbed up a fence in the dark quadrangle.

The doll's arm hung on a small wreath.
I looked up at the building and saw a narrow

square of gray sky, *Did someone jump?*

                            and ran.

THERE WERE PLENTY

We took a toy boat out to the beach;
in a cluster of puddles and vacant crow-shells.

I asked Father, "Where is the white sand?"
He said, "This is a fisherman's beach."

Dried octopi lined weathered nets. Some were grilled.
He opened a beer and sat with the fishermen's wives.

Sister and I climbed the embankments. Stones
trundled in our sandals with beetles like
black thumbs without nails.

"Mr. *Kuro* is on board!" I screamed.
The boat sailed straight.   After two waves, it flipped.

A beetle's legs balanced as if on a rising sea staircase.
"The first funeral," Sister said.

THURSDAYS

1.
Mother cleans
Grandfather's apartment. She picks up a photo
documentary; Auschwitz.
"A heavy, dusty book," she calls it.

                         I ask her, "Will I go to war?"
Holding a vacuum cleaner, she says,
                         "I want your pain." In the smallest
room, my sister cries, her growing teeth.

2.
Grandfather watches TV on the highest volume,
the howling-wind.

He lost his voice seventeen years ago,
stroke. This mouth, and the quietness—
like the people in those black and white photos.

3.
Piles of Jewish clothes, glasses, and hair,
half-naked bodies and holes in the ground,
their stark tongues with dirt in their mouths.
A last word adheres to their throats.

4.
After the atomic bomb in Hiroshima,
Grandfather stood alone on a black hill.
He saw nothing but smoke.
Burnt skin hanging from arms.

Under the August sky, his mother
listened to an imperial speech from a radio.
Japan was lost. Mud beneath her finger nails.

Miles away from home,
he listened to that speech. A stranger
gave him a towel.

A white towel. He wiped his face.
It smelled like dandelions; mother's hands.

IMPOSSIBLY LONG

A big chunk of goat cheese sat on my plate.

Grandfather said,
"If you don't finish it, you cannot start dinner."

The asparagus was impossibly long on the golden fork.
Its strings got caught between my teeth.

The table was crowded with my parents,
cousins, grandmother, and baby sister—

Grandfather proudly told me,
"This restaurant only accepts ten Chinese people a day…"

But we are Japanese.

"It does not matter," he replied.

Roast beef sank in my stomach
on the way back to the hotel.

My frostbitten ears fell off on the eighth street. I kept
gazing at Grandfather's enamel shoes.

We walked

and walked on the cobblestone street

with a glimpse of Paris gray,
living under foreign skin.

AUGUST MARBLE

The charm slopes down from its chain, time passes
like a marble in a *ramune*-soda jar, before
taking it out and rolling it along a channel. The marbles trapped
a dark moss where lunar craters shined,
I told Sister on the last day of August, and gave her one
from my pocket. She said, "I saw two men kissing."
On the jagged rocks, I squinted my eyes
as a satellite would look for new life. She held my arms
and whispered, "Wait for me fifteen minutes,"
then ran back to a corridor. On a Thursday afternoon,
I killed one hour gazing at the marble, searching for the lost men.
Sunlight dried out the lightning bugs among other things.

FATHER'S RÉSUMÉ

Too salty, his death would be like Mother's omelet,
scramble eggs Father loves. Eggshells

walk backward. I carefully
scoop them with a strainer.

Father says, "I will knock on every door."
Mother says, "No, you won't."

I do not know   selling non-stick
frying pans are his dream, coughing up copper.

Peppers, mushrooms and onions slide off on telephone
books and stale beer.   Father
has the longest nap at the library before his body goes to the hospital.

HIS IVORY DIE

#3: additional / seizures after his brain / surgery, #5: broken / front teeth from diabetes… /
Father throws / his ivory die on the floor / I say, #4: "You may die within three / years,
you know?" / he flaps /yesterday's newspaper #2: because his tears / blur out an article
about a comet —even after a star / dies, #6: it may linger as a white / dwarf— I hear / the clatter
of dishes and silverware #1: I push / his wheelchair / the die rolls into a corner of the dining
room / silken layers of stardust cover it / he scoops / egg-drop soup into his mouth.

BRAIN BARCODES

His skull in zip-locks,
all the plastic has barcodes like

two-pound sugar bags, scented
Japanese oranges. Mother's nails dig.
Sister pouts, *What about my wedding?*

Father dribbles. He wears a diaper
Sister and I bought on Tuesday.

By the way,
my fiancée has bladder cancer.

Father lies down in the aisle while a groom
carries a colostomy bag.

Ladies and gentlemen, please raise your glass!

HE USED TO READ TO US "HOW TO DIGEST FOOD"

1.
It was a children's book but not an appropriate one for raising a poet.

2.
Nothing I can do.

3.
One of the Buddhist doctrines is "nothing."
Father wants to change his name into *Kuukan*: the view of nothing.

4.
Father does not eat food for three weeks.

5.
Sister eats an apple, strawberry ice cream, fried rice, teriyaki salmon, tomato,
and a ham sandwich, fairies appear and start their long journeys in the
tunnels.

6.
There were various fairies who dressed up as superstars like *Madonna*,
a sumo wrestler, fisher, runner, pianist, mother with two daughters, and
plumber.

7.
Father is *Kuukan* on the hospital bed, attached to seven tubes.

8.
"A runner carries ice cream because he wants to digest it before it melts.
The superstar, *Madonna* is unhappy after stepping on the droppings with her
high heels," Father said.

9.
Oops.

10.
I said, "It is ok, Father— *Madonna* carried her suitcases behind her."

Sister said, "But *Madonna* needs a stall to change her clothes."

11.
The stall is a cancer cell.

12.
Father had surgery to cut out one mile of intestine.
Mother did not tell me because I am a partial American.

PROCESSING TIME

Great-great grandmother had green tea with me,
took a nap, and passed away shortly after

as if she waited for me to stamp
her final stage of paperwork—

estimated processing time: one hundred and six years;
meanwhile, count the bristles on the railing.

Wanna die?

I smell   meat
grilling in someone's backyard, how hungry I am.

THE COLDEST DAY IS FOR BEANS

A bumble bee hive swayed;
never seen them flying. Sleet
hid the oval shape.

Grandmother lit kitchen stoves
and kerosene-oil heaters.
Azuki-beans drained in the strainer.

No sugar yet. Bitterness must be gone.
I changed the water
and placed them back into the pot.

All windows fogged.
Cooking air condensed.
                    Can I add now?

She curled her back and fell asleep.
Her forehead touched the tatami-mattress.

GREEN APRON

She wears a faded
apron and always eats

pickled Japanese radishes

grains of rice

or oranges

but she is losing her weight
for the paulownia casket

no ash from her bones

she writes sales slips; no letters
with her worm-like hand

her parchment fingers

she gave me a lump of sugar

no expiration date for sugar
it conceals my tongue

and tastes bitter

like falling ash
from a cremation

sunlight bakes the blue blinds
a sugar jar in a Chinese cabinet

she still writes the slips, worries about money

in the smallest kitchen
the smallest island

where I was born

MUGWORT'S LEAVES

Three days before his death,
Are you itchy?

The green-brown liquid,
mugwort's leaves
he boiled them to make lotion.

He cut aloe leaves open.
The veins were sticky.

It may cure when you marry,
He gave me ice-cream.

I curled up in the fur closet. They
repelled water; geese cut through flakes

flying in the February sky.
I scraped my cheeks. My nails split.

VISITING HOURS

Better to die now.
He finally stops lying in front of the TV

yelling at Grandmother

and drops the remote control.
Chopsticks are heavy.

The dark pupils in his shrinking eyes evaporate.

He wants me to stroke his back
like Grandmother does.
I remember her sobbing on the phone.

She wanted a divorce;
instead scrubbed his bathtub for sixty-seven years.

The refrigerator abandoned
fried oysters caked in salt,
sake, and rotten cabbage. Unpaid bills.

FEBRUARY 9, 1919 – NOVEMBER 9, 2008

Shigeru, the old name,
whittled in incense. Chrysanthemums

and orchids shrouded the corpse,
laid on an iron board at a crematorium.

A monk gave him a posthumous Buddhist name,
written in poor calligraphy on a memorial tablet.

When the oven was opened,
I touched his limp cheeks.

Grandmother placed two stones
from an *igo*-board with his glasses.

At another oven, a little boy called,   *Papa,*
a woman held him from falling into it.

Ovens rang as if an elevator
chimed at the last floor.

His skull, cracked sternum,
and a titanium joint between his femur and shin;

his bowels perched.
One stone rested. His melted glasses.

I picked up the remnants;
scalded my fingertips.

EMPTY SHELLS IN VINEGAR

Can you sleep with Grandfather's bones?
Grandmother reaches for a strainer.

Clams quiet in salt water. I steep
the empty shells in vinegar.

It eats through the gray surfaces   ghosts
under the fluorescence.

I pierce a hole.
Are you making shell earrings?

She wears a stained apron;
a uniform for this life.

Lime juice drips on grilled mackerel.
The spinach shrivels

with sesame seeds and sweet soy sauce.
His throat remains in the oven.

Shells rattle;
some crush,

a meteor shower
bursts onto the dining table. Chatterers.

MEADOWSWEET, KOI KOKORO

1.
Every summer, Grandfather wore
geta-slippers   a gap
between his big toes and the others.

He kept telling me the same story. He sold
cloth and met a surveyor in China, 1944.

       Meadowsweet in a Japanese room.

His voice in a cold January wind,
stars flood with blue campanula mornings.

You turn in bed.

I feel your feet.
The warmth,   I wanted it when I was seventeen.

2.
Grandmother sent me a poem
written by an Indian ink stick rubbed on an inkstone
after forty-nine days of mourning.

"I couldn't write my *koi kokoro* to test the ink for color."

Koi kokoro is love
written with a single stroke   like Japanese calligraphy.

Covering colors with colors from a paint brush
kills the art.

You leave
wet paint

purple with yellow dots.   I hate them.

3.
The surveyor had a bound foot
because he wore *geta*-slippers when he was young.

Deep maple forests and meadowsweet in his mind,
he was afraid of showing his Japanese feet in China.

        When Grandfather died,
Grandmother dressed him in a mourning *kimono*.
but she couldn't put him in socks.   His toes were too Japanese.

Since the funeral,
she wears his socks when she goes to bed.

She wants the warmth that I have.

4.
      In Grandfather's diary,
the surveyor fell in love with a Chinese nurse.

She rubbed his foot
under the ink-blotting sky. The early

spring starts to arise after several strokes.

5.
Crystal-clear February ice.   I shout,

"Don't ask me to make love when I write,"
then break every tea cup.

KOTOBUKI, SEVEN PILLOW CASES

Twelve days after we purchased
a queen size bed, Mother

cries on the phone asking,
Do you have pillow cases?

She means seven pillow cases: pink
silk, green satin, white cotton...

Under the sheets, I think of her. Naked
pillows were knocked to the floor Thursday afternoon.

There is no kotobuki in your marriage,
Mother still cries. She wanted to wrap

the pillow cases in thin white
paper and kotobuki: the wedding

symbols of gold
wires made of turtles & cranes; to keep

her busy enough to forget;
I'm leaving her Japanese home.

Mrs. Nakamura showed her pillow cases...
Her daughter married a Nagoya-

born pharmacist. We went to the same
elementary school but I didn't jump

rope with them. I sat on the top of the jungle
gym and conceived of

a veil: snowflakes
in the blue spring.

Kotobuki means happiness and congratulations (blessing) from immediate
family and friends.

MY FIRST MARRIAGE

is killing itself, but
it is not my fault. Your hidden bottles under
the book shelf, honeymoon suitcase. Empty
whiskey. When you want to eat ground beef, I stir
the frozen meat into miso soup, and hysterically
commit plates (maybe partially my fault) to a dump. If
I earn enough money, if I bring a box of brown
rice to the table, if I pay rent.   If my
marriage is a green-card, I am not
overdosing on painkillers. You
watch TV and then the cat, in turn, says,
"Be aware of my cocoon period, Darling."

FUJIMOTO   **KASZA**

My last name and yours
never pulled
our kinetic   pubic hairs,
beetles smeared;
stabbed.

"Yes (comma) I do."

We jumped without a hyphen
—sweetie, you are not
a bird. Your short arms.
Twenty-four thousand feet;
geese laugh at two floaters.

IN LAWRENCEVILLE; HONEYMOON

Time and again; time   and again; I sit
        and stay in my Japanese body; no

honeymoon: no
dining table: eight months and three

thousand dollars an Asian
or Pacific Islander resident.

Immigrant; it's pending: I can do
nothing: I am

nothing until it clears; *I can't hire you*
secretaries treat me as   an illegal

alien,   warn my red
passport will expire soon. I smack

a laundry basket into a chair   I feel
accomplished in this country; in Lawrenceville,

Illinois: two
blocks down from a Catholic church: we rent

an apartment   behind a gas station.

HOW TO CHOKE MYSELF IN THE UGLY KITCHEN

I stumbled on the kitchen floor
in a counterclockwise wonderland

colorful macaroons and a mouthful of sherbet. Dried

skin flaked in my long hair. It covered
my lineless back moles.

Sweetie, he called
without kissing my forehead.

He drilled a hole and hung a phone from the 1970s,
and painted the wall in puke.

I shoveled instant coffee into my mouth.

> There is

an extra season of endless fields.
The postcard fell from the refrigerator.

Sweetie, from behind a leather couch.
The TV remote abandoned on the carpet.

I wiped my hands with a paper towel and said, *I am here*.

THE PERCH SHED THEIR SILVER

I pour oil, fry perch,
mince onions and carrots,

                    drowning in a car. Fists

bang on the windshield.
I haven't turned off the stove.

My eyeballs float
loosed lily-balloons.

Brahms' Rhapsody numbs
my brain.

The perch shed their silver
in an upright piano.

No scales. No
Japanese name

squeezes out of my throat. I forget
I was once in Mother's womb.

My lungs
resign.   Smoke alarm. I burned the fish.

WELCOME HOME

A gigantic kiwi swallows this room,
black and white tiles and concrete walls.
I heard a prison's punishment room is this color,
as is its laundry room, and underneath the dryer
smells like piss. "Welcome to our home"
haunts our eyes in this torture chamber.
The previous owner was an old lady
who passed away in a hospice eighteen months ago.
She might have had an animal or two,
or a big one. Their cages might have been in this room.
The raw meat squelched. Her last word was, "Share."
I bought a lime scented spray,
and am scrubbing the floor with it until
you close the windows. Three
patches of light disappear. Smells of goat. First house.

AISLE TWENTY CENTURY

A woman shelved boxes: *My baby is not graduating high school.*
When she was nineteen, she had a son: *It's his decision, you know?*

Freckles cover her nose:
The price doesn't matter, the same result.

She hands me two pink boxes: *Buy one, get one free.*

Smile.

Overnight frostbite killed the geraniums.
A cradle with flower printed sheets is on sale here.

I don't know.

I do not know
if I am even right to be a mother at a right time.

DIVIDING

1.
Grandfather met a pregnant woman, summer 1945.

She held an empty bottle and a little red *kimono*
      and sat down by a gray fence.

He gave her water

      and kept walking to the hill near Hiroshima
      and then bullets rained

      and the bomb.

2.
He found her again,
a shred of red cloth.

Her bowels
      and placenta spread

under the fence; in a ditch.

He did not find her unborn child, but smelled it.

3.
      How beautiful the spring of 1946 was;

dandelions and clovers covered the fence.

4.
Millions of cells divide
in amniotic bubbles;

a new heart pumps in my womb.

       And you ask,
"Do we give it a Japanese or American name?"

Does not matter—

I will stroke its forehead every night,

humming an old lullaby.

BEFORE THE SUNSET

Your skipping-stone glides around
as if a flying fish crosses
from ocean to ocean, shines its scales.

The ocean fills up with acerbic sentiments.
You give me the smoothest, the best kind of skipping-stone.
I throw horizontally but it dives and splashes.

The waves ripple. My tears dribble into the ocean.
I wasted your stone.   I waste another stone.
But when you find a new one and hold it in my hand,

our palms lie together like a bivalve.
It carries a pearl-grey summer.
Before sunset, I skip my stone again.

Lamps come on in a house;
Stars fragment the western sky
behind our path to the bridge.

MORE THAN FOURTEEN DAYS

Because there is no answer,
beetles roll,
ants dismantle.

An ideal summer
shines more than fourteen days.

Unwrapped pacifiers. Ghost
teeth bite my nipples.   Things
live without purpose, nor dreams like

a fly prays on a watermelon; its forelegs
sticking. I don't need nine months. I need

groceries—
eggs, tomatoes, cilantro, maybe bell peppers.

JUNE INK

The kitchen dyed
empty green like a milk glass.
A feeding bottle drifted out on turbulent waves.

Mother told of a miscarriage hidden from me

for twenty-eight years.

Her tears dripped on the newspaper;
paragraphs and paragraphs of rain blotted

I smelled June ink instead. On that day,
a French airplane disappeared in the Atlantic Ocean.

A passenger held a baby-girl.
They saw shattered windows falling.

LAKE MICHIGAN

No clam's bubbles to step on the lake beach.
Waves just come and go— no seaweed, no fisherman's nets.
Plastic caps tumble, but no bead coral.
Lifeguard's freckled shoulders. Nobody screams, "Jellyfish!"
Wind tosses my hair across my mouth.
I taste nothing like standing by the seashore near a beach house— rusted roofs.
You sweated and wanted to name the baby, *"Yume."*
I said, *"Dream?"* and I did not like it. Too ephemeral white.
                    Clouds stretch.
Maybe you knew— first breath, almost.

DOVE SOAP,

Mother's smell.
She held me, radiating a heavenly

aura. Saints in religious art
carried a halo of holy light.

Prickly grains of salt
a crescent lime

abused my lips,
tongue. A stubborn artist scribbled

the plaster into my throat, stomach.
I drained half a gallon of colors

sank into a fluorescent
pink-green margarita.

A scab peeled the harsh outline of my face.
She was in a lemon nightgown when I left.

PHOBOS AND DEIMOS

Two moons;
non-mothered sky.

I traced his wrinkled pajamas with my forefinger.
My earlobes glued to his back.
I heard his heart   a metronome

the constant light
            tapping from thousands of years ago;

a chameleon liquidized, eggs on its tongue.

FROM AN APARTMENT

Smashed sticky chewing gum;
I smell stale beer,
a recycling box,

crows, electric wires,
trembling camphor trees.

Mother. *Step back!*

Buses honk at   yellow cabs.
The drivers' eyes follow me,

mannequins.
Black street lamps stick
toward the cloudless sky.

I tiptoe down the crosswalk
by the fountain of polished granite.

Yesterday's newspaper
drowns in it. *Kurumamichi Station.*

NECESSARY DEVELOPMENT

A dog barked. Somebody slammed their door shut.
Excavators shook.

Are you ready to leave Japan?
M smiled and the train doors closed.

Her passport and *gaijin*-card occupied her purse.

Grandfather had never known life after March 11th.
I took the train to his graveyard

and saw a woman like her—
a head taller than the other commuters.

We met at the vegetarian noodle shop,
around the corner of a narrow parking lot.
New camellias bloom.

THE FIRST NIGHT
after the tsunami on 3/11/2011

1.
When I was eight years old, I squatted
down in a futon-closet & waited
for my mother. My aunt opened
the closet with wheat bread

  & eight boiled eggs.

2.
Dear Mother,
Did you escape the land of sudden

  death?

3.
I waved my hands to the silver
whistles of a helicopter in the morning
sky. It dropped a rope like a spider thread

  three miles away from my tree.

4.
A little yellow shoe drifted away. I
clasped my hands around the tree
trunk & smelled

  the water desert.

MISO SOUP
after the tsunami on 3/11/2011

Men shovel dirt and rubble.
Under this heavy clay,

they find a street.

The tsunami siren blows.
They run up to the hill   again.

> I walked behind Father
> and listened to earthworms on wet leaves.
> "We don't sit on a swing today," he said,
>
> so I stared at his moving feet.

A man asks,
"Keep digging for what?"

This street does not take us home.

> In her kitchen, Mother cooked miso-soup;
> mushrooms and tofu on the cutting board,
> slice of salmon on the grill.

The windows are clouded with steam.

Under the moonlight in the sea,
thousands of ghosts migrate.

They scatter seeds on the street.

Shovels glimmer.

The most beautiful flowers bloom
under the broken swing.

REQUIEM FROM AN OFFICE 7,000 MILES AWAY
after the tsunami on 3/11/2011

I type numbers and sit in a black
chair for eight hours. Glass cloth
covers my eyes. Cold
sand fills my bones. A graveyard

on the hill is burning.

After the earthquake, a fisherman
runs to the fire. He carries
a clarinet and yells to me,

What else do you want?

My eyelids are sealed like wax stamps.
A tsunami pushes the flaming tombstones and boats.

Under the white moon, the fisherman
plays a clarinet concerto. He vibrates
the reed. In the ocean breeze, he inhales
human dust. I open

my eyes. I want

lights

and then more lights.

EYELASHES, FOUR

1.
A *tsunami*
crashes onto my eyelashes;

a million   leaping waves into the sky.

A white basin clogs
then I see your headlights from the window.

2.
I need more salt;

salt enough for cleansing my hands
          and body.

Water is still running   running from the spigot.

3.
Tonight, you take me from the rusty place
          and your blue wagon parks by the creek.

Cold   June night breezes stroke my eyelashes.
I hear laughter from a cracked spigot.

4.
My eyelashes   branch out to the sky.

Their tips tangle with Orion's Belt
          and turn into early summer   seaside gentians.

GREENHOUSE

The foreign sky is; my frozen marrow:
Mother's blood, carrots: *her carrot cake*, the crumbs
scattered on the range and shears: *sharp shears* tangled
with a steel kettle; it was the spell to find lost needles
after she sewed a skirt: *my gingham skirt*, the needles
pierced Father's eyeballs; his pallid tie: no job;
his record player played *Debussy*; the rusty sprinklers,
the snail escaped and I cowered in the shrubs of rhododendron:
in the ever-green greenhouse; Mother
listened to a music box: the foreign gray.

I STOLE HIS ADAGIO

The records stood in three rows
on his bookshelf, which came from his college dorm
and Mother hated.

He wanted to live in the past;
lumps of sugar, a drop of milk in a breakfast tea,
an ephemeral pledge with dark eyes, unlike Mother's.

He sat on his couch
while Mother prepared the tea
and laundered his shirts. The dryer spun,

the kettle squeaked, and the music turned louder.
But soon,
Mother screeched and flapped the shirts.

She pulled out the plug; he flung the newspaper,
and I hid under the dining table,
every Sunday morning.

In my quiet apartment, I remember him.
My phone rings. The Adagio clanks.

SAKURA, SAKURA, CHERRY BLOSSOM

I was waiting for the railway crossing. On the radio,
guitarists played an old Japanese folk song
that was an early spring surprise. When I closed
my eyes, I could see cherry blossoms at *Tokugawa Park*.
They were budding for a long time, and then
suddenly gray-pink petals fell
and yellow stamens covered the streets.
I picked up the blossoms and pressed them
in telephone books before rain-drops ruined
these now transparent beautiful
existences, and I always handed the best to Mother.
I do not remember when I walked through
the tree-lined road last time. I forgot
the lyric................The car behind me honked.
A couple of snowflakes landed on the windshield.

LEAF BLOWERS

"You will die shortly. Wear anything you want,"
I say to Grandmother and launder her black shawls.

A ghost swaddles her emerald broach.
Her shoes dim like young nails.

Piles of paper cut out Grandfather's face.

After his funeral, I lay under the piano.

Your fingers trill the keys;
leaf blowers reverberate my skull.

Hails bullet the soil.

If you die first, I have no idea—
for example, the cable television bills, its password,

and a complete set of crap.

More doorbell rings. A truck
drops off boxes.

Your un-fertilized descendants carry them to the dumpster.

STEPS ON THE BRICK

I told Mother my cat brought me a baby bird.
She said her grandson caught a gigantic blue butterfly.
"Look at me!" He did not use his mouth. Stealthy steps.
His little palms together. Its feelers bent,
so did the bird's spirit on the first day falling from the nest.
I do not have a child, but I wonder
what this mother feels. Death of little things.
The bird cuddled by the corner of the window,
oozing out its shit. Eyes wide open, unfocussed.
The cat stared at it, not eating nor playing,
just observing, as if asking, "Aren't you gonna die?"
I closed the curtains.   Next morning,
the bird left white steps on the brick. I try to believe it flew away.

GRAPE FLAVOR

After he showed me his blue locomotive,
Takuma said, "This is the fastest," his small body
kneeling over the rails from a wool rug,
a Yubari-melon box station, a big styrofoam elephant
standing guard. He sat in front of it,
sold me a one-way ticket and a doughnut, "Grape flavor."

The train ran under a pink trunk, cords
crossing sockets. "I need to charge"
he wrapped them around his wrist and neck
as if he commanded electricity like
an absolute creature in this carpet society.

"Stop it," I said, his shoulders startled. He twisted
his body twice and looked at the web-camera,
wiggled his arms to tighten it. I said, "Don't."

I grabbed my stuffed toy and hitched a rope.
"It chokes you, you die."   "Mommy,"

he blustered over the television-phone,
crying and overflowing with tears, "Don't be angry."
I was tired stuffing imaginary doughnuts, one after another.
So I closed with only one thing, "I am your Aunt." Sister
turned off the screen so they could walk to the park.

SEVENTEEN BLUE IN MY MAIL BOX

The cranes crowd.

Seventeen blue origami
scatter on the floor. Buddha folds
one more for my *shiawase*.

        What did you expect?

Mother rings a bell
from her wheelchair. I change her diaper.

A sudden noise
comes from Buddha's stomach.

He brings me an apron. I open
the refrigerator and reheat
steamed rice and smoked mackerel.

From the plates,
he feeds Mother and the paper

birds.   I wring

their necks.

JAPANESE APRICOT WINE

The cloudy nebula spreads.
It tastes good this year.

I open Mother's last bottle
in a dark corner of the kitchen cabinet.

I pray   stars
stars scatter in her breasts
vaporize the swelling.

Cosmic dust falls into Jupiter. The apricot pit
hollows out her sheets.
Nurses remove Mother's name.

THE PAY PHONE

"I want to live,"
her voice didn't go through.

Her funeral was forty-six days
after she left for the hospice.

Purple and luminous,
a galaxy in darkened space.

A single page of an unfinished letter
and a cup of chamomile tea on a desk.

I sit down on her bed
and push my forehead into her pillow;

smells of her neck.

The concrete road,
spots slowly absorb the whole universe taking her arms,

lost breasts.

WHISPERS OF SILVER-GRASS

Two thousand years ago,
a sleepless Japanese poet sings

a song of a carbonated moon
on a decaying boat with tangled dragnets
separating his wife and two daughters.

Whispers of silver-grass
like still unreachable silk holograms
illuminate human hearts— are
his family, maybe mine too.

HER GARDEN ON FIFTH FLOOR

1.
Yes, Mother. I'll be home by 7:00 pm.

> There is a traffic jam and my red
> bicycle is stolen at a subway station.

No, Mother. It isn't today.
> That's when I moved to another country.
> I'm home seventeen years later at 7:00 pm.

In her city, nobody can point toward Elkhart.

2.
Dandelions smell like the hands of a five-year-old.

I liked when she pushed my back on a swing
one early yellow May.
Then we picked up Sister's birthday cake.

> *Yes, Mother. I know how to go back home.*

3.
When I close my eyes—
I'm walking on the streets by willow trees.
Her balcony appears between those branches.

Azaleas are about to bloom and surround
> the stepping stones sinking in a sea of moss.

4.
Sister and I
found the silver sheen of snails after June rain in her Japanese garden.

TRIP TO ANOTHER DIMENSION

It is not hard to lose a map,
even though she writes me one
from the station to home

and stitches it on my left kneecap. She eats
a cookie on her father's thigh in a train.
The crumbs disappear

after three stations. Her father tucks
in her hair like a bead curtain, like her red sari—
it bandages her legs. She carries

dirt from a truck to the railroad during the summer.
She stirs a bottle of lemon dregs and plays an accordion
one corner past the busiest station, so I

listen to it for two blocks
while tasting coffee grounds. I have not
lost my location yet—aging for sure, the window shows

my sunken cheeks. If I disappear into another
dimension, I look at an aperture and tell her,
"I am a patient."

(cancer perhaps) her strawberry
ice-cream melts,
drips on her shoes in a gentle gradient.

Note:

I am grateful to Indiana University South Bend. Nancy Botkin, Kelcey Parker Ervick, and David Dodd Lee who taught me through their creative writing courses. Respect to all my colleagues and professors; especially, Yoshiko Green and Joe Chaney. During my college semesters, Amanda Groendyke and Kathy Plodowaski proofread my writings.

Nanzan Junior College is always in my heart. Merryn Black, Bill Kumai, Natsuko Awamura, Akiko Amano, Momoe Adachi, and Mizuho Fujiyoshi. It was the happiest and most innocent time of my life.

I was so happy to have met Elizabeth & Leif when I was seventeen.

I am thankful to have communities— RHINO Poetry, the Tupelo Press 30/30 Project, and allow me to have friendships with Angela Narciso Torres, Silvia Bonilla, and Dara Elerath.

Love to my families; especially, my husband who proofreads all my poems and encourages me to keep writing in English. I love you, Aaron.

Thank you very much to Aquarius Press/Willow Books, Randall Horton and Heather Buchanan, who believe in my work.

Thank you very much to you who always support my poetic career.

Acknowledgements:

Gratitude to the following journals for publishing, some in different forms: *Alchemy Magazine of Literature & Art, Anti-, Big Scream, the Birds We Piled Loosely, Chiron Review, Cider Press Review, Construction Literature Magazine, Epiphany a Literary Journal, Gargoyle Magazine, Hotel Amerika, Jet Fuel Review, Juked, Moria, Natural Bridge, New Madrid, POETRY, Passages North, Prairie Schooner, Puddle Lake Review, Puerto del Sol, Spillway,* and *Tupelo Press 30/30 Anthology.*

About the Poet

Naoko Fujimoto was born and raised in Nagoya, Japan. An exchange student, Naoko received a B.A. and M.A. from Indiana University. A RHINO associate editor, her **Naoko Fujimoto Poetry & Art** site introduces readers to graphic poetry, showcases books and project developments and shares other influential poets and their accomplishments.